Friend to Friend

Helen Steiner Rice

R Revell
A DIVISION OF
Baker Book House Co

FRIEND TO FRIEND
by Helen Steiner Rice

© 1993 by Virginia J. Ruehlmann and
the Helen Steiner Rice Foundation

Originally published under the title *This
Is the Day: A Daily Devotional* (calendar) by Gibson Greetings Inc.

© 1995: Christian Art, P.O. Box 1599,
Vereeniging, South Africa

Designed by: Christian Art

ISBN 0-8007-7146-X

Friend to Friend

Helen Steiner Rice

Revell
A DIVISION OF
Baker Book House Co

FRIEND TO FRIEND
by Helen Steiner Rice

© 1993 by Virginia J. Ruehlmann and
the Helen Steiner Rice Foundation

Originally published under the title *This
Is the Day: A Daily Devotional* (calendar) by Gibson Greetings Inc.

© 1995: Christian Art, P.O. Box 1599,
Vereeniging, South Africa

Designed by: Christian Art

ISBN 0-8007-7146-X

Not only on New Year's,
but all the year through,
God gives us a chance to
begin life anew.

*Lord, I have heard of your fame;
I stand in awe of your deeds,
O Lord. Renew them in our day,
in our time make them known.*
Habakkuk 3:2 NIV

This is the day to start anew.
With the beginning of a
new year, plan a personal
renewal as well.

As the new year starts
and the old year ends,
There's no better time
to make amends
For all the things
we sincerely regret
And wish in our hearts
we could somehow forget.

*For if you truly amend your
ways and your doings, ... then I
will let you dwell in this place.*
Jeremiah 7:5-7

This is the day to bid farewell
to the year just ending and
welcome the new one with its
challenges and opportunities.

All of God's treasures
are yours to share
If you love Him completely
and show Him you care.

*We love, because he
first loved us.*
I John 4:19

This is the day to put another
log of friendship on the fire
and kindle the embers when
you sense a chill between
two neighbors.
Acting as a peacemaker
is one of God's greatest
treasures.

Accept what the
new year brings,
Seeing the hand of God
in all things,
And as you grow in
strength and grace,
The clearer you can
see God's face.

*Both riches and honor come
from thee, and thou rulest over
all. In thy hand are power and
might ...*
I Chronicles 29:12-13

This is the day to marvel as you
discover a bit of God in people,
in antur and in happenings.

Suddenly, Lord,
I'm no longer afraid,
My burden is lighter,
and the dark shadows fade.

Cast your burden on the Lord,
and he will sustain you;
he will never permit the
righteous to be moved.

Psalm 55:22

This is the day to
dismiss all negative
thinking and concentrate
on the positive.

You make me feel welcome,
You reach out Your hand,
I need never explain,
for You understand.

Welcome one another, therefore,
as Christ has welcomed you,
for the glory of God.
Romans 15:7

This is the day to welcome
Christ into your home and
your heart.
Your home and heart should
always have the welcome
mat displayed.

We all make mistakes,
for it's human to err,
But no one need ever
give up in despair,
For God gives us all
a brand-new beginning,
A chance to start over
and repent of our sinning.

*Who is a God like you,
who pardons sin and forgives
the transgression of the
remnant of his inheritance?*
Micah 7:18 NIV

"I'm sorry" can sound like
music to the ears of the one
wronged.

As you start another year,
May you feel His presence near,
And may happiness
that's heaven-sent
Fill your heart with joy
and content.

*Surely you have granted him
eternal blessings and make him
glad with the joy of your
presence.*

Psalm 21:6 NIV

This is the day to apply
yourself wholeheartedly to the
year ahead and its tasks. The
only place that success comes
before work is in the dictionary.

Whatever the new
year has in store,
Remember, there's
always good reason for
Everything that comes
into our life,
Even in times of
struggle and strife.

*My son, do not make light
of the Lord's discipline,
and do not lose heart
when he rebukes you.*
Hebrews 12:5 NIV

This is the day to remove
strife from your life by adding
giving to your living.

Only love can make man kind,
And kindness of heart
brings peace of mind,
And by giving love
we can start this year
To lift the clouds
of hate and fear.

Jesus answered him, "If a man loves me, he will keep my word, and my Father will love him, and we will come to him and make our home with him.

John 14:23

You can give yourself a lift by
raising the level of
kindness which you extend.

Everybody everywhere,
no matter what his station,
Has moments
of deep loneliness
and quiet desperation.

We are hard pressed on every side, but not crushed; perplexed, but not in despair, persecuted, but not abandoned; struck down, but not destroyed.
2 Corinthians 4:8 NIV

This is the day to visit a friend either in person or by telephone.

For things that cause
the heart to ache
Until we feel that it must break
Become the strength by which
we climb to higher heights
that are sublime.

*Therefore do not be anxious
about tomorrow, for tomorrow
will be anxious for itself. Let the
day's own trouble be sufficient
for the day.*
Matthew 6:34

This is the day to help someone
up the hill of life. Be a
facilitator, an encourager.

Lord, I'm unworthy, I know,
but I do love You so –
I beg You to answer my plea …
I've not much to give,
but as long as I live,
May I give it completely
to Thee!

*Give heed to me, O Lord, and
hearken to my plea.*
Jeremiah 18:19

This is the day to dedicate
your future to your Lord,
to give Him your present
and to offer up your past.

Make me a channel
of blessing today,
I ask again and again
when I pray –
Do I turn a deaf ear to
the Master's voice
Or refuse to heed
His directions and choice?

*Here I am! I stand
at the door and knock.
If anyone hears my voice and
opens the door, I will come in.*
Revelations 3:20 NIV

This is the day to follow
the Master's directions.
Listen to His voice.

Take a cup of kindness,
mix it well with love,
Add a lot of patience
and faith in God above.

*And whoever gives to one
of these little ones even a
cup of cold water because he is
a disciple, truly, I say to you,
he shall not lose his reward.*
Matthew 10:42

This is the day to
develop kindness.
It is closely related to
greatness and adds to the
enjoyment of living for you
and those around you.

Start every day with a
"good morning" prayer
And God will bless each thing
you do and keep you in His care.

*Every day I will bless thee,
and praise thy name for
ever and ever.
Great is the Lord, and
greatly to be praised, and his
greatness is unsearchable.*
Psalm 145:2-3

This is the day to make your
mornings good, your noons
better and your nights best
by placing them in God's care.

In Thy goodness and
mercy look down
on this weak, erring one
And tell me that I am forgiven
for all I've so willfully done.

If we confess our sins,
he is faithful and just,
and will forgive our sins
and cleanse us from all
unrighteousness.
I John 1:9

This is the day to hold
yourself accountable to the same
standards you demand of others.

Hour by hour and day by day I talk to God and say when I pray, "God, show me the way so I know what to do, I am willing and ready if I just knew.

And I heard the voice of the Lord saying, "Whom shall I send, and who will go for us?" Then I said, "Here am I! Send me."

Isaiah 6:8

This is the day to realize that every problem has a solution and every solution has a beginning. Ask God to make you part of the solution.

How will you use
the days of this year
and the time God has
placed in your hands –
Will you waste the minutes
and squander the hours,
leaving no prints behind
in time's sands?

*Behold, now is the acceptable
time; behold, now is the day
of salvation.*
2 Corinthians 6:2

This is the day to think
of time as a gift from God.
Appreciate each second.

Although we're unworthy,
dear Father above,
Accept us today
and let us
dwell in Thy love.

I can do all things in him
who strengthens me.
Philippians 4:13

This is the day to seek
residence in God's love
and to invite Jesus
to reside in your heart.

Keep on believing,
whatever betide you,
Knowing that God will
be with you to guide you,
And all that He promised
will be yours to receive
If you trust Him completely
and always believe.

*I will praise you forever for
what you have done; in your
name I will hope, for your name
is good.*
Psalm 52:9 NIV

This is the day to display a faith
that remains unshaken despite
the onset of tribulations.

Try to live a little better and
always be forgiving –
Add a little sunshine to the
world in which we're living.

*Then Peter came up and said to
him, "Lord, how often shall my
brother sin against me, and I
forgive him? As many as seven
times?" Jesus said to him, "I do
not say to you seven times, but
seventy times seven."*

Matthew 18:21, 22

This is the day to warm the
lives of those around you by
your Christlike attitude.

There are many things in life
we cannot understand,
But we must trust
God's judgment
and be guided
by His hand.

But he trusted to him who
judges justly.
1 Peter 2:23

This is the day to face
your problems with the
understanding that God has
hidden a blessing
within each problem.

I come not to ask, to plead
or implore You –
I come just to tell You
how much I adore You,
For to kneel in Your presence
makes me feel blessed,
For I know that You know
all my needs best.

*Blessed be the Lord! for he
has heard the voice of my
supplications.*
Psalm 28:6

This is the day to
listen to your heart.
Each beat is a thank-you
note to God.

Thank you again for
Your mercy and love
And for making me heir
to Your kingdom above!

The Lord is my strength and
my shield; in him my heart
trusts; so I am helped, and my
heart exults, and with my song
I give thanks to him.

Psalm 28:7

This is the day to
contemplate your relationship
with the Lord.

All who have God's blessing
can rest safely in His care,
For He promises safe passage
on the wings of faith and prayer.

*I long to dwell in your tent
forever and take refuge in the
shelter of your wings.*
Psalm 61:4 NIV

This is the day to proceed on
life's journey by travelling
with God as your co-pilot.

Whatever our problems,
our troubles and sorrows,
If we trust in the Lord,
there'll be brighter tomorrows.

*I trust in the steadfast
love of God for ever
and ever.*

Psalm 52:8

This is the day
to be content in the
knowledge that
God knows best.

I said a little prayer for you,
and I asked the Lord above
To keep you safely in His care
and enfold you in His love.

If you abide in me, and my
words abide in you,
ask whatever you will, and it
shall be done for you.
John 15:7

This is the day to experience
God's presence as you pray
for those you love.

Faith in things we cannot see
Requires a child's simplicity –
Oh, Father, grant
once more to men
A simple, childlike
faith again.

For we walk by faith,
not by sight.
2 Corinthians 5:7

This is the day to
confide in Christ.
Tell Him your faith is
childlike, and your trust
has matured.

Open up your hardened heart
and let God enter in –
He only wants to help you
a new life to begin.

*Don't grumble against each
other, brothers,
or you will be judged.
The Judge is standing
at the door!*

James 5:9 NIV

This is the day to answer
your heart's door chime.
God is waiting. Ask Him in.

When God forgives us,
we too must forgive
And resolve to do better
each day that we live
By constantly trying to be
like Him more nearly
And trust in His wisdom
and love Him more dearly.

*Bear with each other and
forgive whatever grievances you
may have against one another.
Forgive as the Lord forgave you.*
Colossians 3:13 NIV

This is the day to imitate Jesus.
Forgive someone who has hurt
you. Turn the other cheek.

"Love one another as
I have loved you"
May seem impossible to do,
But if you will try
to trust and believe,
Great are the joys that
you will receive.

*I have told you this so that my
joy may be in you and that your
joy may be complete.*
John 15:11 NIV

This is the day to be a living
sermon for the people in your
life. It is far more meaningful
for them to see a sermon
than to hear one.

After the night, the morning,
bidding all darkness cease,
After life's cares and sorrows,
the comfort and sweetness
of peace.

The Lord is your keeper;
the Lord is your shade on
your right hand.
The sun shall not smite you by
day, nor the moon by night.
Psalm 121:5-6

This is the day to thank your
Creator for your hopes, your
dreams and your faith
in what is to come.

God, how little
I am really aware
Of the pain and the trouble
and deep despair
That flood the hearts of
those in pain
As they struggle to cope
but feel it's in vain.

Wait for the Lord; be strong,
and let your heart take courage;
yea, wait for the Lord!
Psalm 27:14

This is the day to look beyond
the behavior of that unpleasant
individual. Analyze why the
unkind words were spoken.
Be understanding.

God, in Thy great wisdom,
lead us in the way that's right,
And may the darkness
of this world
be conquered by Thy light.

*I have come as light into the
world, that whoever believes in
me may not remain in darkness.*
John 12:46

This is the day to recharge
your spiritual generator.
Request the Light of the world
to illuminate your way.

Let me stop complaining
about my load of care,
For God will always lighten it
when it gets too much to bear.

*When the cares of my heart are
many, thy consolations cheer
my soul.*
Psalm 94:19

This is the day to handle
yourself by using your head.
Handle others by using
your heart.

May you find comfort
in the thought that
sorrow, grief and woe
Are sent into
our lives sometimes
to help our souls to grow.

*The law of the Lord is perfect,
reviving the soul.*
Psalm 19:7

This is the day to cultivate
an attitude of assistance.
If a neighbor experiences a
sorrow, be the first one to ask,
"What can I do to help?"

The Lord is our salvation and
our strength in every fight,
Our redeemer and protector,
our eternal guiding light.

*Come, let us walk in the
light of the Lord.*

Isaiah 2:5

This is the day to protect
someone's reputation if you
hear malicious gossip.
Guide the conversation
to a higher level.
Discourage rumors.

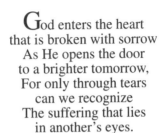

God enters the heart
that is broken with sorrow
As He opens the door
to a brighter tomorrow,
For only through tears
can we recognize
The suffering that lies
in another's eyes.

Why are you cast down,
O my soul, … Hope in God; for
I shall again praise him, my
help and my God.
Psalm 43:5

This is the day to improve
self-esteem in an individual
who is lacking it.

Earthly pain is never too much
When He bestows
His merciful touch,
And if you look to Him and pray,
He will help you
through every day.

For whatever is born of God
overcomes the world;
and this is the victory that
overcomes the world, our faith.
I John 5:4

This is the day to avoid
complaining. Appreciate
even the smallest of courtesies
extended to you.

It does not take a special time
to make a brand-new start,
It only takes the deep desire
to try with all our heart.

*But he who looks into the
perfect law, the law of liberty,
and perseveres, being no hearer
that forgets but a doer that acts,
he shall be blessed in his doing.*
Jame 1:25

This is the day to exchange
some negative habits
for more productive ones.
Put them into action.
Practice and persevere
at being a doer!

There's no need at all
for impressive prayer,
For the minute we seek God,
He is already there!

*Pray to your Father who is in
secret; and your Father who
sees in secret will reward you.*

Matthew 6:6

This is the day to engage
in pleasant conversation
with God.

After the clouds, the sunshine,
after the winter, the spring,
After the shower, the rainbow,
for life is a changeable thing.

*Whenever I bring clouds over
the earth and the rainbow
appears in the clouds, I will
remember my covenant between
me and you and all living
creatures of every kind.*
Genesis 9:14-15 NIV

This is the day to change
someone's life by acting
as a rainbow.

Love makes us patient,
understanding and kind,
And we judge with our hearts
and not with our minds,
For as soon as love enters
the heart's open door
The faults we once saw
are not there anymore.

Love must be sincere.
Romans 12:9 NIV

This is the day
to bring out the best in
another person.

Love is like magic,
and it always will be,
For love still remains
life's sweet mystery!

*God is love. Whoever
lives in love lives in God,
and God in him.*
I John 4:16 NIV

This is the day to influence
someone's life by
demonstrating the magic
of love; after all, it is love that
makes the world go 'round

Shed Thy light upon us
as Easter dawns this year,
And may we feel the presence
of the risen Savior near.

The Lord has risen indeed.
Luke 24:34

This is the day
to rise above the pettiness
that is prevalent in
society today.
Let your own light shine.

He who walked by the Galilee
Touched the blind and
made them see
And cured the man who
long was lame,
When they but called God's
holy name.

*Then the eyes of the blind
shall be opened, and the ears
of the deaf unstopped; then
shall the lame man leap like
a hart, and the tongue of the
dumb sing for joy.*
Isaiah 35:5-6

This is the day to strive to
do something constructive.
Put forth an effort to right
a wrong.

Take me and break me
and make me, dear God,
just what you want me to be –
Give me the strength
to accept what you send
and eyes with the vision to see.

*But the Lord stood by me and
gave me strength to proclaim
the message fully.*
2 Timothy 4:17

This is the day to possess
a vision of hope.
Apply action to your dream.
With God's help it will
come to fruition.

Teach us to take time
for praying
and to find time
for listening to You,
So each day is spent well
and wisely doing what You
most want us to do.

*Watch and pray that you may
not enter into temptation; the
spirit indeed is willing, but the
flesh is weak.*
Matthew 26:41

This is the day to prioritize your
responsibilities. Be well-
adjusted spiritually, physically,
mentally and emotionally.

Trouble is something
no one can escape,
Everyone has it
in some form or shape.

Then they cried to the Lord in
their trouble, and he saved them
from their distress.

Psalm 107:13 NIV

This is the day
to value the existence
of trouble.
It strengthens
your coping skills.

Uncover before me
my weakness and greed
and help me to search
deep inside
So I may discover how easy it is
to be selfishly lost in my pride.

Pride goes before destruction,
and a haughty spirit
before a fall.
Proverbs 16:18

This is the day
to be concerned about others.
Plan to serve God first,
then others and then yourself.

I wish I could wipe away
every trace of pain and
suffering from your face,
But He is great
and we are small,
We just can't alter
His will at all.

*He will wipe away every tear
from their eyes, and death shall
be no more, … for the former
things have passed away.*
Revelation 21:4

This is the day to enjoy a
beauty treatment. Remove the
frown from your face
and add a smile.

Never give up in despair and
think that you are through,
For there's always a tomorrow
and a chance to start anew.

*You, were taught, with regard to
your former way of life, to put
off your old self, which is being
corrupted by its deceitful
desires; to be made new in the
attitude of your minds; and to
put on the new self, created to
be like God in true
righteousness and holiness.*
Ephesians 4:22-24 NIV

This is the day to learn from
each person you meet and from
each happening.

Just keep on smiling,
whatever betide you,
Secure in the knowledge
God is always beside you.

*I smiled on them when they had
no confidence; and the light of
my countenance they did not
cast down.*

Job 29:24

This is the day to share the
secret of a truly happy life.
Encourage the talent within
a youngster.

God has promised
to sustain us,
He's our refuge from all harms,
And underneath this refuge
are His everlasting arms!

*The eternal God is your
dwelling place, and underneath
are the everlasting arms.*
Deuteronomy 33:27

This is the day to study a
crucifix. Observe that even on
the cross Christ's arms are open
wide in welcome.

My cross is not too heavy,
my road is not too rough,
Because God walks beside me,
and to know this is enough.

*When you pass through the
waters I will be with you; and
through the rivers, they shall not
overwhelm you; when you walk
through fire you shall not be
burned, and the flame shall not
consume you.*

Isaiah 43:2

This is the day to
travel the rough roads
and traumatic times
with God beside you.

Though I'm tired and weary
and I wish my race were run,
God will only terminate it when
my work on earth is done.

I have fought the good fight,
I have finished the race,
I have kept the faith.
2 Timothy 4:7

This is the day to polish your
trophy called compassion, a
humanitarian award conceived
by God for those who alleviate
the suffering of others.

Miracles are all around
Within our sight
and touch and sound,
As true and wonderful today
As when the stone
was rolled away.

*… they asked each other,
"Who will roll the stone away
from the entrance of the tomb?"
But when they looked up, they
saw that the stone, which was
very large, had been
rolled away.*
Mark 16:2-4 NIV

This is the day to put your
shoulder to the stone
of indifference.

Seed must be sown
to bring forth grain,
And nothing is born
without suffering and pain.

*Now he who supplies seed to the
sower and bread for food will
also supply and increase your
store of seed and will enlarge
the harvest of your
righteousness.*
2 Corinthians 9:10 NIV

This is the day to reap
that which you have sown.
Did you plant seeds
of kindness?
Then harvest a bushel
of kindnesses.

When our lives are overcast
with trouble and with care,
Give us faith to see beyond
the dark clouds of despair.

*Therefore I tell you, do not be
anxious about your life.*
Matthew 6:25

This is the day
to mature and grow in grace.
The sun is hiding behind the
clouds, and your frown is a
smile turned upside-down.

Flowers sleeping peacefully
beneath the winter's snow
Awaken from their icy grave
when spring winds start to blow.

So we do not lose heart.
Though our outer nature is
wasting away,
our inner nature is being
renewed every day.
2 Corinthians 4:16

This is the day to look for and
discover hidden possibilities.
Bring out the dormant potential
within another person.

Be glad that you've walked
with courage each day,
Be glad you've had strength
for each step of the way,
Be glad for the comfort
you've found in prayer,
But be gladdest of all
for God's tender care.

Be glad in the Lord, and rejoice.
O righteous, and shout for joy,
all you upright in heart!
Psalm 32:11

This is the day to stroll
with a confident air.
Jesus is at your side teaching
you to walk as He walked.

The bleakness of the winter
is melted by the sun.
The tree that looked so stark
and dead becomes a living one.

*Water will gush forth in
the wilderness and streams
in the desert.*
Isaiah 35:6 NIV

This is the day to melt any
hardness in your heart.
Reach out in forgiveness.
Life goes on.

May I stand undaunted
come what may,
Secure in the knowledge
I have only to pray
And ask my Creator
and Father above
To keep me serene in His
grace and His love!

And whatever your ask in
prayer, you will receive,
if you have faith.
Matthew 21:22

This is the day to remain
calm in the face of
all adversities.

How can man feel
any fear or doubt
When on every side,
all around and about.
The March winds blow
across man's face
And whisper of God's
power and grace.

*By his wind the heavens
were made fair.*
Job 26:13

This is the day to renew
your amazement at the
power and majesty of God.
It is no secret what
He can do.

God, be my resting place
and my protection
In hours of trouble,
defeat and dejection,
May I never give way
to self-pity and sorrow,
May I always be sure
of a better tomorrow.

Every word of God proves true;
he is a shield to those who take
refuge in him.
Proverbs 30:5

This is the day to use all
twenty-four hours to make the
most of yourself, because there
will never be another you.

God, open my eyes so
I may see and feel
Your presence close to me,
Give me strength
for my stumbling feet
As I battle the crowd
on life's busy street.

*For now we see in a mirror
dimly, but then face to face.
Now I know in part; then I shall
understand fully, even as I have
been fully understood.*
1 Corinthians 13:12

Do not concentrate on the
physical features, but rather the
inner beauty. Are you
pleased with what you see?

Widen the vision
of my unseeing eyes,
So in passing faces
I'll recognize
Not just a stranger,
unloved and unknown,
But a friend with a heart
that is much like my own.

*Then turning to the disciples he
said privately, "Blessed are the
eyes which see what you see!*
Luke 10:23-24

You cannot judge a book by its
cover, and do not judge a person
by the garments being worn.

Love works in ways that are
wondrous and strange,
And there is nothing in life
that love cannot change,
And all that God promised
will someday come true
When you love one another
the way He loved you.

*Now remain in my love. If you
obey my commands, you will
remain in my love, just as I have
obeyed my Father's commands
and remain in his love.*
John 15:9-10 NIV

This is the day to treat all those
with whom you have contact as
you wish they would treat you.

Happiness is giving up wishing
for things we have not
And making the best
of whatever we've got –
It's knowing that life
is determined for us
And pursuing our tasks
without fret, fume or fuss.

There is great gain in godliness
with contentment; for we
brought nothing into the world,
and we cannot take anything
out of the world.
1 Timothy 6:6-7

This is the day to do the job
assigned to you really well.

Let us face the trouble
that is ours this present minute
And count on God to help us
and to put His mercy in it.

*The Lord disciplines
those he loves.*
Hebrews 12:6 NIV

This is the day to introduce
the word "help" into
your vocabulary.
Help yourself,
help others,
and thank God
for His help.

By completing what God
gives us to do,
We find real contentment
and happiness too.

For the sake of Christ, then,
I am content with weaknesses,
insults, hardships, persecutions,
and calamities; for when I am
weak, then I am strong.
2 Corinthians 12:10

This is the day to look for the
many available opportunities
to serve God.
Don't wait for big, exceptional
chances, but use small,
daily occasions.

Enjoy your sojourn
on earth and be glad
That God gives you a choice
between good things and bad,
And only be sure
that you heed God's voice
Whenever life asks you
to make a choice.

Today, if you hear his voice,
do not harden your hearts.
Hebrews 3:7-8 NIV

This is the day to banish
gloom and add cheer to
somebody's life.
Replace sadness with
gladness.

God's love knows
no exceptions,
so never feel excluded –
No matter who or what you are,
your name has been included.

*Let your face shine on your
servant; save me in your
unfailing love.*
Psalm 31:16 NIV

This is the day to discover
the really important things
in your life.

Forget the past and future
and dwell wholly on today.
For God controls the future,
and He will direct our way.

*There is a future for the
man of peace.*
Psalm 37:37 NIV

This is the day to call to
mind the saying,
"Today is the first day of
the rest of your life."

Give me perception
to make me aware
That scattered profusely
on life's thoroughfare
Are the best gifts of God
that we daily pass by
As we look at the world
with an unseeing eye.

*But, as it is written, "What no
eye has seen, nor ear heard,
not the heart of man conceived,
what God has prepared
for those who love him."*

1 Corinthians 2:9

This is the day to describe the
sunrise or sunset to someone
who cannot see it.

Our Father who art in heaven,
hear this little prayer,
And reach across
the miles today
that stretch
from here to there.

Our Father who art in heaven,
Hallowed be thy name.
Matthew 6:9

This is the day
to write a letter of
affirmation
to someone.

Happiness is waking up
and beginning the day
By counting our blessings
and kneeling to pray.

Happy the people to whom
such blessings fall!
Happy the people whose
God is the Lord!

Psalm 144:15

This is the day
to wake up singing
and improve your outlook.

God, grant us grace to use
all the hours of our days
Not for our own selfish interests
and our own willful ways.

*And he came to the disciples
and found them sleeping;
and he said to Peter,
"So, could you not watch
with me one hour?"*
Matthew 26:40

This is the day to be helpful.
You will find that the degree
of happiness you achieve is
directly related to the degree
of helpfulness you offer.

Life's lovely garden would
be sweeter by far
If all who passed through it
were as nice as you are.

*For lo the winter is past, the
rain is over and gone.
The flowers appear on the
earth, the time of singing has
come, and the voice of the
turtledove is heard in
our land.*

Song of Solomon 2:11-12

This is the day
to meet Jesus in the garden.
Walk and talk with Him.

In the glorious Easter story
a troubled world can find
Blessed reassurance
and enduring peace of mind.

And he said to them, "Do not be
amazed; you seek Jesus of
Nazareth, who was crucified. He
has risen, he is not here, see the
place where they laid him."

Mark 16:6

This is the day to harmonize
with nature's orchestra. Crickets
chirp, brooks babble, flowers
and trees sway to the rhythm of
the symphony of praise to our
Savior. Even thunder adds
a clap of applause.

Our Savior's resurrection
was God's way of telling men
That in Christ we are eternal
and in Him we live again.

For this is the will of my Father,
that every one who sees the
Son and believes in him
should have eternal life;
and I will raise him up
at the last day.
John 6:40

This is the day to rejoice
in the realization
that our earthly cares and
sorrows are minimal when
compared to the reward of
eternal life.

Everything worth having demands work and sacrifice, And freedom is a gift from God that commands the highest price.

It is for freedom that Christ has set us free. Stand firm, then, and do not let yourselves be burdened again by a yoke of slavery.
Galatians 5:1 NIV

This is the day to value the freedoms you enjoy daily.

My blessings are so many,
my troubles are so few,
How can I feel discouraged
when I know that I have You.

Be strong and courageous.
Do not be terrified; do not be
discouraged, for the Lord your
God will be with you
wherever you go.
Joshua 1:9 NIV

This is the day to display a
spiritual magnetism.
Attract others to Jesus
by your example of a
positive faith.